Weekly Reader Books presents
Tuff Stuff

A Children's Book about Trauma

by

Joy Wilt

Illustrated by Ernie Hergenroeder

Educational Products Division
Word, Incorporated
Waco, Texas

Author

JOY WILT is creator and director of Children's Ministries, an organization that provides resources "for people who care about children"—speakers, workshops, demonstrations, consulting services, and training institutes. A certified elementary school teacher, administrator, and early childhood specialist, Joy is also consultant to and professor in the master's degree program in children's ministries for Fuller Theological Seminary. Joy is a graduate of LaVerne College, LaVerne, California (B.A. in Biological Science), and Pacific Oaks College, Pasadena, California (M.A. in Human Development). She is author of three books, *Happily Ever After, An Uncomplicated Guide to Becoming a Superparent*, and *Taming the Big Bad Wolves*, as well as the popular *Can-Make-And-Do Books*. Joy's commitment "never to forget what it feels like to be a child" permeates the many innovative programs she has developed and her work as lecturer, consultant, writer, and—not least—mother of two children, Christopher and Lisa.

Artist

ERNIE HERGENROEDER is founder and owner of Hergie & Associates (a visual communications studio and advertising agency). With the establishment of this company in 1975, "Hergie" and his wife, Faith, settled in San Jose with their four children, Lynn, Kathy, Stephen, and Beth. Active in community and church affairs, Hergie is involved in presenting creative workshops for teachers, ministers, and others who wish to understand the techniques of communicating visually. He also lectures in high schools to encourage young artists toward a career in commercial art. Hergie serves as a consultant to organizations such as the Police Athletic League (PAL), Girl Scouts, and religious and secular corporations. His ultimate goal is to touch the hearts of kids (8 to 80) all over the world—visually!

This book is a presentation of Weekly Reader Books.
Weekly Reader Books offers book clubs for children from
preschool through junior high school.

For further information write to:
WEEKLY READER BOOKS
1250 Fairwood Ave.
Columbus, Ohio 43216

Tuff Stuff

ISBN: 0-8499-8136-0
Library of Congress Catalog Card Number: 79-50045

Janet Gray, Editor

The educational concepts presented in the Ready-Set-Grow book series are also featured in a music songbook and longplay record. For further information concerning these materials see your local bookstore or write Word, Incorporated, 4800 West Waco Drive, Waco, Texas 76710.

Contents

Introduction

<u>Tuff Stuff</u> is one of a series of books. The complete set is called *Ready-Set-Grow!*

<u>Tuff Stuff</u> deals with difficult experiences that children might have to go through. This book can be used by itself or as a part of a program that utilizes all of the *Ready-Set-Grow!* books.

<u>Tuff Stuff</u> is designed so that children can either read the book themselves or have it read to them. This can be done at home, church, or school. When reading to children, it is not necessary to complete the book at one sitting. Concern should be given to the attention span of the individual child and his or her comprehension of the subject matter.

<u>Tuff Stuff</u> is designed to involve the child in the concepts that are being taught. This is done by simply and carefully explaining each concept and then asking questions that invite a response from the child. It is hoped that by answering the questions the child will personalize the concept and, thus, integrate it into his or her thinking.

Tuff Stuff teaches that while life may go smoothly most of the time, at some point in every person's life, he or she will have to face situations that are very difficult to handle. They might result from a person's making a mistake or doing something wrong, or they might happen to a person through no fault of his or her own.

When a difficult experience causes a person deep and lasting pain, that person is going through trauma. But even though trauma is upsetting, it can help a person to learn a great deal about himself or herself and the world, to grow, and to become a better person—if it is handled properly.

Tuff Stuff is designed to equip children with constructive techniques for handling difficult and painful situations. Children who grow up having these skills will be better equipped to live healthy, productive lives.

Tuff Stuff

Life goes smoothly most of the time, but not all the time.
Sometimes life gets pretty rough.

If people could choose just how their lives would be, everyone would probably want to be healthy, happy, and safe all the time.

But no one has ever been healthy, happy, and safe all the time.

Sometimes unpleasant things happen.

Everyone—no matter who he or she is, how old he or she is, what he or she has, or where he or she lives—has unpleasant experiences.

Sometimes these unpleasant experiences cause trauma.

Chapter 1

What Is Trauma?

Sometimes, when your body gets hurt, you feel terrible at first . . .

but soon you stop hurting.

Sometimes, when your feelings get hurt, you're very unhappy at first . . .

but soon you feel better.

But sometimes, the hurt doesn't go away so easily.

You might feel angry, sad, lonely, and scared.

You might think nobody loves you anymore.

You might think something terrible is going to happen to you.

You might think you're a bad person.

You might think you'll never be happy again.

If something happens that hurts your feelings or body and makes you feel very bad for a long time, you're probably going through trauma.

The things that cause trauma are called traumatic experiences.

Why do people have traumatic experiences?

Sometimes, when people experience trauma, it's their own fault.

If you break rules that are made for your good and the good of other people, or if you do something dangerous, you might have a traumatic experience.

SPUNKY WAS VERY OLD.
HE HAD A LONG, HAPPY
LIFE.

I GUESS HE HAD TO DIE
SOMETIME. I GUESS IT
WASN'T MY FAULT,
WAS IT?

But sometimes people have traumatic experiences through no
fault of their own.

Many different kinds of experiences can cause trauma. The next chapter will tell you about some of the traumatic experiences that you may go through at some time or another.

Chapter 2

Traumatic Experiences That You Might Have

NIGHTMARES

The thoughts and pictures you have while you're sleeping are called dreams.

If a dream is frightening, it is called a nightmare.
Having a nightmare might make you go through trauma.

This is Elizabeth. Elizabeth used to have a lot of nightmares.
Her nightmares made her feel . . .

scared, trapped, weak, and helpless.

Elizabeth's nightmares made her wonder:

33

Elizabeth figured out that every time she watched a scary movie just before she went to bed, she had a nightmare. So she doesn't watch scary movies anymore.

She also won't listen to scary stories.

NOT ME. I WANT TO SLEEP TONIGHT!

HEY ELIZABETH! WHERE ARE YOU GOING? DON'T YOU WANT TO WATCH DRACULA?

Before she goes to sleep, Elizabeth checks her room to make sure it's safe. She locks the windows so nothing can get in, and she leaves the door open so she doesn't feel trapped.

She thinks about something pleasant that she would like to dream about.

Now Elizabeth hardly ever has nightmares.

SEPARATION

If you leave someone you care about . . .

or if someone you care about leaves you, you might go through trauma.

This is Douglas. Douglas's parents left him with his grandmother while they took a vacation. This made Douglas feel . . .

angry, sad, left out, jealous, and lonely.

When Douglas's parents left him, Douglas thought:

While his parents were gone, Douglas kept busy doing things he enjoyed. He met some new friends.

When he missed his parents, he talked with his grandmother about how he felt.

He wrote letters to his parents, and they sent him picture postcards almost every day. He marked on a calendar the day they were coming home.

All these things helped Douglas to feel much better about being separated from his parents.

MOVING

If you move from one house to another . . .

or if you change schools, churches, or clubs, you might go through trauma.

This is Grant. Grant's father got a new job in a faraway town, and Grant's family had to move. This made Grant feel . . .

angry, frustrated, sad, nervous, anxious, and scared.

48

When Grant had to move, he thought:

Grant's mother showed him a map of the town where they were moving. He found out where their new house was, where he would be going to school, and where there were parks and playgrounds.

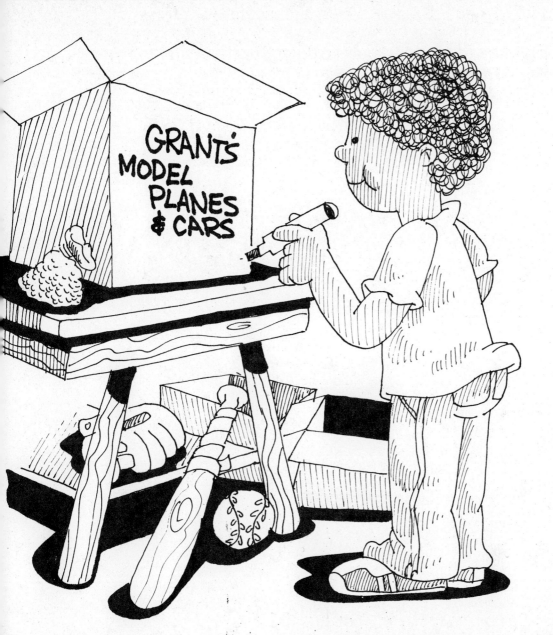

Grant packed his own clothes and toys.

His dad took a picture of all his friends standing together, and they gave Grant their addresses.

These things helped Grant to feel much better about moving.

ADDING A NEW PERSON TO THE FAMILY

If somebody moves into your house . . .

or if a new baby is born or adopted into your family, you might go through trauma.

This is Emily. Emily's mother and stepfather had a baby boy,
and Emily felt . . .

SIGH!

jealous, threatened (afraid the baby
might take her place), and left out.

56

After the new baby was born, Emily thought:

THEY SURE ARE CRAZY ABOUT LITTLE ERIK. I BET THEY DON'T EVEN THINK ABOUT ME ANYMORE.

Emily decided to talk with her parents about how she felt.

58

Emily learned how to help take care of the baby.

She and her parents arranged special times to spend together without little Erik.

All these things helped Emily to feel much better about having a baby brother.

DIVORCE

When a husband and wife decide they don't want to be married anymore, they get a divorce . . .

and stop living together. Divorce can make everyone in a family go through trauma.

This is Karen. Karen's parents got a divorce. Karen felt . . . angry, rejected (unwanted), unloved, sad, and lonely.

After her parents' divorce, Karen thought:

65

Karen wrote letters to her father.

Karen helped her father plan what they would do during the time they spent together.

Karen was glad her parents didn't fight with each other any longer.

These things help Karen to feel better about her parent's divorce.

VISITS TO THE DENTIST, DOCTOR, OR HOSPITAL

If you have to visit a dentist's or doctor's office . . .

or go to the hospital, you might go through trauma.

This is Gerald. Gerald had to go to the hospital to have his tonsils taken out. This made Gerald feel . . .

insecure (unsure of what was going to happen to him), scared, and worried.

Before Gerald went to the hospital, he thought:

Gerald decided to find out everything he could about the hospital. He read books and asked questions.

74

When Gerald went to the hospital, he took things he liked to do. He asked his parents to come see him as often as they could.

When his throat hurt, he talked to the nurse about how he felt.

All these things helped Gerald to feel much better about being in the hospital.

INJURIES

If you hurt yourself . . .

or if someone else hurts you, you might go through trauma.

This is Jack. Jack broke his arm while he was playing football.

When the accident happened, Jack's arm hurt a lot, and he was scared.

Afterward, he felt angry and lonely.

Jack found out he could still do fun things, even though his arm was in a cast.

He was careful not to do anything that seemed too dangerous.

Jack's friends offered to sign his cast and draw on it.

These things helped Jack to feel much better about having a broken arm.

DISABILITIES

A condition of the body that prevents a person from doing things most people can do is called a physical disability.

A condition of the mind that prevents a person from doing things most people can do is called a mental disability.

If you don't understand disabilities, seeing disabled people can make you go through trauma.

This is Gwen. Gwen lives close to a school for disabled children. This makes Gwen feel...

uncomfortable, curious, and judgmental.

Seeing a person who is disabled makes Gwen think:

Gwen decided to find out everything she could about disabled people. She read books and asked questions.

DISABLED PEOPLE ARE SPECIAL AND IMPORTANT, JUST LIKE EVERYONE ELSE. THEY HAVE FEELINGS, AND THEY NEED TO BE LOVED AND RESPECTED, NOT PITIED.

Gwen got to know some of the disabled children who went to the school near her house.

Her new friends explained to her how they became disabled.

ROGER WAS BORN WITH HIS LEGS AND ARMS CROOKED. MARY HAS A DISEASE THAT MAKES HER WEAK. AT FIRST I COULDN'T UNDERSTAND HER WHEN SHE TALKED, BUT NOW I CAN.

These things helped Gwen to feel much better about disabilities.

DEATH

When a person finds out that he or she is very sick and might not live very long, he or she goes through trauma.

When a person dies, his or her friends and relatives go through trauma.

This is Cindy. Cindy's grandmother died, and Cindy felt . . .

sad, angry, scared, and lonely.

Cindy thought:

At first Cindy tried to pretend she didn't care that her grandmother had died. But one night she cried very hard for a long time.

Cindy drew pictures of everything she remembered about her grandmother.

She thought about her happiest memories of her grandmother.

All these things helped Cindy to feel better about her grandmother's death.

All of these experiences can cause trauma:

Nightmares

Separation

Moving

Adding a new person to the family

Divorce

Visiting the dentist, doctor, or hospital

Injuries

Handicaps

Death

Some of these experiences might happen to you many times, while others may never happen to you.

Have you gone through any of these experiences?

If so, how did you feel?

What did you think?

What did you do?

Has anything else happened to you that caused you trauma?

How did you feel?

What did you think?

What did you do?

Traumatic experiences are always unpleasant. But if you handle them carefully, you can . . .

learn about yourself, other people, and the world; grow; and become a better person.

Chapter 3

Handling Trauma

No matter what causes trauma . . .

there are several things you can do to help yourself feel better and
to learn from your experience.

Step 1: Face it. Figure out what caused the trauma and face up to it. Don't try to pretend it didn't happen.

When Cindy's grandmother died, Cindy had to face it.

Step 2: Accept it. Try to get used to the way things are.

Cindy had to accept her grandmother's death.

Step 3: Figure out if anything you did caused the traumatic experience. Sometimes you do things which bring on trauma; sometimes you do not.

Think about it.

Cindy had to figure out whether she made her grandmother die.

Step 4: Decide what you are going to do about the traumatic experience, and if there is anything you can do, do it.
Sometimes you can do something to change things, sometimes you can't.

Step 5: Do what you have decided to do.

Cindy had to decide what she would do about her grandmother's death.

117

Step 6:   Talk about your thoughts and feelings. You will have many feelings and thoughts. Don't keep them inside you. Share them with someone else.

Cindy talked about her thoughts and feelings.

Keep talking about your thoughts and feelings for as long as you need to. Don't think that talking about a traumatic experience one time will make everything okay. It might take you as long as six months, or even a year, to feel better and get all your questions answered.

When you talk to someone about your thoughts and feelings, make sure . . .

you have time to talk and the other person
has time to listen,

the person you talk to cares about you and
might be able to help you, and

you tell the other person exactly how you
feel and what you are thinking.

Following these steps can help you learn and grow, so that even though a traumatic experience is painful, good things can come from it.

Conclusion

Every person, no matter who he or she is, no matter how old he or she is, what he or she has, or where he or she lives, will go through traumatic experiences some time during his or her life.

A person might have a traumatic experience when he or she breaks a rule or does something dangerous.

Or a person might have a traumatic experience through no fault of his or her own.

Traumatic experiences are upsetting and hard to handle, but if they are handled carefully, they can help a person . . .

learn a lot about himself or herself, other people, and the world; grow; and become a better person.

This is why . . .

The "tuff stuff" that happens to you is important and needs to be handled carefully.